Table Of Contents

I0477804

Chapter 1: Introduction to Pharmaceutical Success

3

Chapter 2: Pathways to Pharmaceutical Success

14

Chapter 3: Building Effective Relationships with Healthcare Providers

22

Chapter 4: Mastering Pharmaceutical Sales Techniques

31

Chapter 5: Navigating Regulatory Compliance in Pharma

41

Chapter 6: Utilizing Digital Marketing Strategies for Pharma Sales

51

Chapter 7: Developing Product Knowledge and Therapeutic Expertise

60

Chapter 8: Enhancing Communication Skills for Medical Representatives

68

Chapter 9: Leveraging Data and Analytics in Pharmaceutical Sales

78

Chapter 10: Understanding Market Access and Reimbursement Strategies

86

Chapter 11: Training and Development Programs for Medical Reps

95

Chapter 12: Exploring Career Advancement Opportunities in Pharma Sales

104

Chapter 13: Conclusion and Future Outlook

112

Thank you for purchasing our book.
We hope you love it!

Inside this guide, you'll uncover expert
strategies and techniques designed to elevate
your sales performance, foster robust
relationships with healthcare professionals,
and expertly navigate the intricate landscape
of the pharmaceutical industry.

Copyrights©

This content is copyright of
Maples Book Solutions© 2024.
All rights reserved.

Chapter 1: Introduction to Pharmaceutical Success

The Role of a Medical Representative

The role of a medical representative is pivotal in bridging the gap between pharmaceutical companies and healthcare providers. Medical representatives serve as the frontline ambassadors of their organizations, tasked with promoting the benefits and features of pharmaceutical products to physicians, pharmacists, and other healthcare professionals. Their ability to communicate effectively and build trust is essential in ensuring that healthcare providers understand the value of medications and therapies, ultimately influencing prescription decisions. This requires not only a comprehensive understanding of the product portfolio but also an awareness of the therapeutic areas they represent, enabling them to address the specific needs and concerns of healthcare professionals.

Building effective relationships with healthcare providers is the cornerstone of a medical representative's responsibilities. Trust and rapport are critical components in the healthcare ecosystem, where providers rely on representatives for accurate information and support. By engaging in meaningful conversations and demonstrating a commitment to ongoing education, medical representatives can position themselves as trusted partners. This relationship-building goes beyond mere transactions; it involves understanding the healthcare provider's practice, their patient demographics, and the challenges they face. Such insights enable representatives to tailor their approach, presenting solutions that align with the provider's needs and ultimately enhancing patient care.

Mastering pharmaceutical sales techniques is another vital aspect of a medical representative's role. This requires a blend of strategic selling, negotiation skills, and an acute awareness of the competitive landscape. Medical representatives must be adept at identifying potential objections from healthcare providers and employing effective counterarguments that highlight the unique selling propositions of their products. Additionally, staying informed about market trends and competitor activities empowers representatives to adapt their strategies and maintain a competitive edge. Continuous training and skill development are necessary to refine these techniques and respond to the dynamic nature of the pharmaceutical industry.

Navigating regulatory compliance is an essential duty that medical representatives need to focus on. The pharmaceutical sector operates under strict regulations that determine how products are marketed and sold. Representatives must have a solid understanding of these regulations to guarantee that all promotional efforts align with industry standards. This approach not only safeguards the reputation of the pharmaceutical company but also promotes transparency and trust with healthcare providers. By following ethical practices and regulatory guidelines, medical representatives can strengthen their credibility and emphasize the significance of responsible marketing in the healthcare field.

In an increasingly digital landscape, leveraging data and analytics has become essential for pharmaceutical sales success. Medical representatives can utilize various digital marketing strategies to enhance their outreach efforts, targeting specific healthcare providers with tailored messaging. Data analytics can provide insights into prescribing patterns, market access challenges, and reimbursement strategies, equipping representatives with the information needed to make informed decisions. By integrating technology into their sales processes, medical representatives can optimize their efforts, measure the effectiveness of their campaigns, and ultimately drive better outcomes for both their organizations and the healthcare professionals they serve.

Overview of the Pharmaceutical Industry

The pharmaceutical industry plays a critical role in the global healthcare landscape, characterized by its complex interplay of research, development, manufacturing, and marketing of medications. This sector is dedicated to discovering innovative solutions that address unmet medical needs and improve patient outcomes. The industry is not only driven by scientific advancements but also influenced by regulatory frameworks, market dynamics, and the ever-evolving landscape of healthcare delivery systems. For sales and marketing representatives, understanding these facets is essential for navigating their roles effectively and establishing impactful relationships with healthcare providers.

Pharmaceutical companies engage in a rigorous research and development process to bring new drugs to market. This journey often spans several years and involves substantial financial investment. From initial drug discovery to clinical trials and regulatory approval, each phase requires specialized knowledge and a keen understanding of scientific and regulatory requirements. Sales representatives must appreciate the intricacies of this process to communicate effectively with healthcare professionals and convey the value of their products. Building a solid foundation of product knowledge and therapeutic expertise enables representatives to engage in meaningful conversations with prescribers, ultimately influencing their prescribing behaviour.

The pharmaceutical industry is significantly influenced by regulatory compliance, which dictates all facets of drug development and marketing. Regulatory bodies like the Food and Drug Administration (FDA) in the United States are crucial in confirming that medications are safe, effective, and manufactured to high-quality standards. Medical representatives need to have a thorough understanding of these regulations to meet legal and ethical obligations while advocating for their products. Grasping the complexities of compliance enables representatives to reduce risks and establish trust with healthcare providers, which is vital for nurturing enduring professional relationships.

In today's digital age, leveraging digital marketing strategies has become imperative for pharmaceutical sales. The industry has witnessed a significant transformation with the advent of technology, allowing representatives to utilize data analytics, social media, and online platforms to reach healthcare professionals effectively. By harnessing these tools, sales teams can not only enhance their outreach but also personalize their communications based on insights derived from data. This shift toward digital engagement facilitates stronger connections with healthcare providers and provides valuable opportunities for education and product promotion.

Career advancement in the pharmaceutical industry is closely linked to ongoing training and development. As the market evolves, so too must the skills of sales and marketing representatives. Participating in training programs focused on enhancing communication skills, mastering sales techniques, and understanding market access strategies is crucial for professional growth. Moreover, fostering a culture of continuous learning within organizations empowers representatives to stay at the forefront of industry trends and best practices. This commitment to development not only benefits individual careers but also contributes to the overall success of the pharmaceutical company in achieving its objectives.

Importance of Effective Sales Strategies

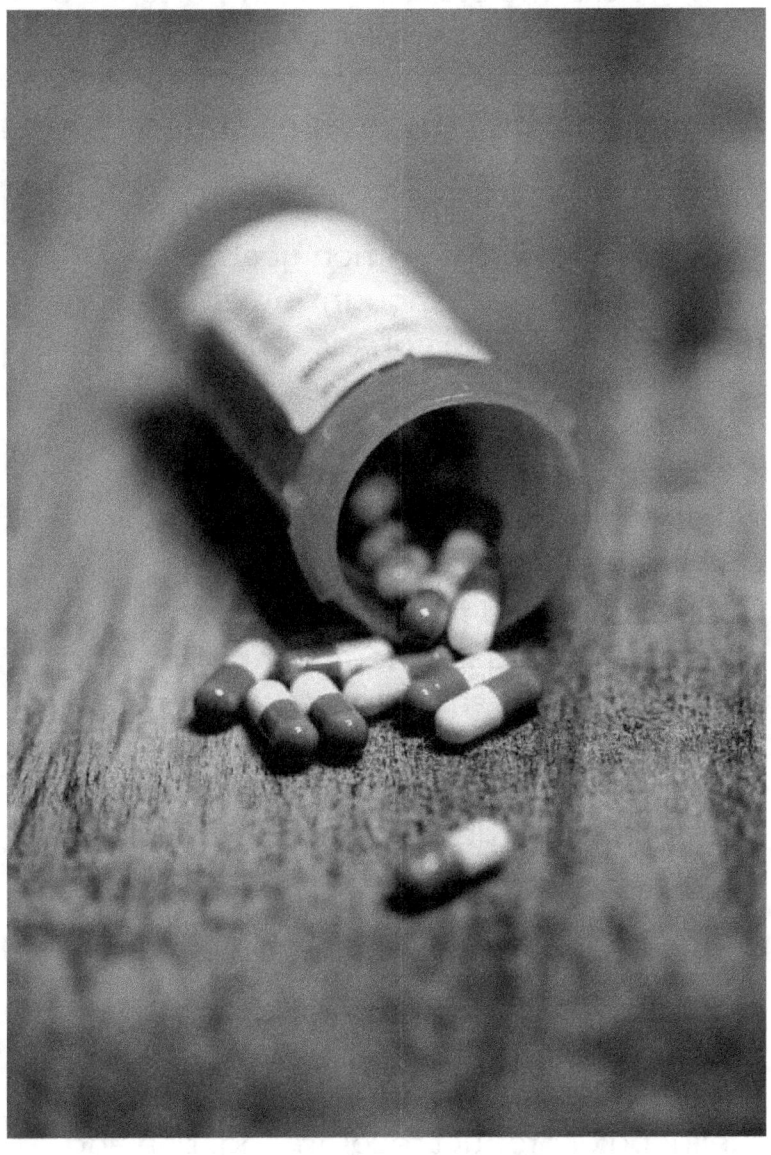

Effective sales strategies are the cornerstone of success in the pharmaceutical industry. For sales and marketing representatives and managers, understanding the importance of these strategies is crucial for achieving sales targets and fostering sustainable growth. Sales strategies not only guide representatives in their day-to-day interactions with healthcare providers but also align the efforts of the entire sales team toward common goals. By implementing well-thought-out strategies, representatives can enhance their ability to communicate product value, thereby improving engagement with healthcare professionals and driving prescriptions.

Building effective relationships with healthcare providers is paramount in pharmaceutical sales. Representatives who employ effective sales strategies can establish trust and credibility with their clients. This involves not just selling a product but understanding the needs and preferences of healthcare providers and their patients. By utilizing tailored approaches that resonate with the specific interests of healthcare professionals, sales representatives can position themselves as valuable partners in patient care, significantly increasing the likelihood of product recommendation and acceptance.

Moreover, mastering pharmaceutical sales techniques is essential for navigating the complexities of the healthcare landscape. Effective sales strategies include knowledge of various selling techniques, such as solution selling, consultative selling, and relationship selling. By mastering these techniques, representatives can adapt their approach based on the context of the conversation and the unique characteristics of the healthcare provider. This adaptability ensures that representatives can effectively communicate product benefits while addressing potential concerns, leading to more successful outcomes.

In the current digital era, utilizing technology via digital marketing strategies is essential for pharmaceutical sales. Successful sales approaches now integrate digital tools that offer insights into market trends, customer behaviours, and competitive intelligence. By employing data analytics and digital platforms, representatives can improve their outreach, focus on specific groups of healthcare providers, and connect with them using tailored content. This enhances the effectiveness of sales initiatives while fostering a more knowledgeable approach to building relationships and promoting products.

Finally, ongoing training and development programs are essential components of effective sales strategies. The pharmaceutical industry is constantly evolving, with new regulations, products, and market dynamics emerging regularly. Continuous education and skill enhancement empower sales representatives to stay current with industry changes and improve their sales techniques. By investing in training, organizations can ensure that their sales teams are equipped with the knowledge and tools necessary to meet the challenges of the market, ultimately leading to greater success in sales performance and career advancement opportunities within the pharmaceutical sector.

Chapter 2: Pathways to Pharmaceutical Success

Understanding the Pharma Sales Landscape

Understanding the pharmaceutical sales landscape is essential for sales and marketing representatives and managers within the pharma industry. This landscape is characterized by rapid changes influenced by technological advancements, evolving regulatory frameworks, and shifting market dynamics. The pharmaceutical sector is not only about selling products; it encompasses a comprehensive understanding of the healthcare ecosystem, including the needs and behaviours of healthcare providers (HCPs), patients, and payers. By grasping these elements, representatives can position themselves strategically to meet the demands of the market while aligning their objectives with the broader goals of their organizations.

At the core of the pharmaceutical sales landscape lies the relationship between medical representatives and healthcare providers. Building effective relationships with HCPs is paramount, as these professionals are often the gatekeepers to patient care and treatment decisions. Success in this realm requires not only product knowledge but also an understanding of the unique challenges faced by HCPs, including time constraints and the need for credible information. Representatives who cultivate trust and demonstrate a genuine commitment to supporting HCPs in delivering quality care are more likely to succeed in fostering long-term partnerships.

The role of regulatory compliance cannot be underestimated in the pharmaceutical sales landscape. Navigating this complex environment requires a solid understanding of the laws and regulations that govern the industry. Compliance is not merely a checkbox; it is integral to maintaining the integrity of pharmaceutical sales practices. Sales representatives must be well-versed in the guidelines that dictate interactions with HCPs, promotional activities, and reporting requirements. This knowledge not only protects the organization from legal repercussions but also enhances the credibility of the sales force in the eyes of healthcare providers.

Digital marketing strategies have emerged as a formidable tool in the pharmaceutical sales landscape. As the industry evolves, so too must the approaches employed by sales representatives. Utilizing digital platforms enables representatives to engage with HCPs in more personalized and meaningful ways. This shift towards digital engagement not only enhances outreach but also allows for targeted communication that aligns with the specific needs and preferences of healthcare providers. Embracing these strategies equips sales representatives with the ability to leverage data and analytics, making informed decisions that can significantly impact their sales performance.

Finally, understanding market access and reimbursement strategies is crucial for navigating the pharmaceutical sales landscape. Representatives must be equipped with the knowledge of how products gain access to the market and the reimbursement processes that influence prescribing behaviours. By comprehensively understanding these strategies, medical representatives can effectively communicate the value of their products to HCPs and stakeholders. This insight not only enhances their credibility but also positions them as valuable partners in the healthcare decision-making process, ultimately driving pharmaceutical success.

Key Competencies for Medical Representatives

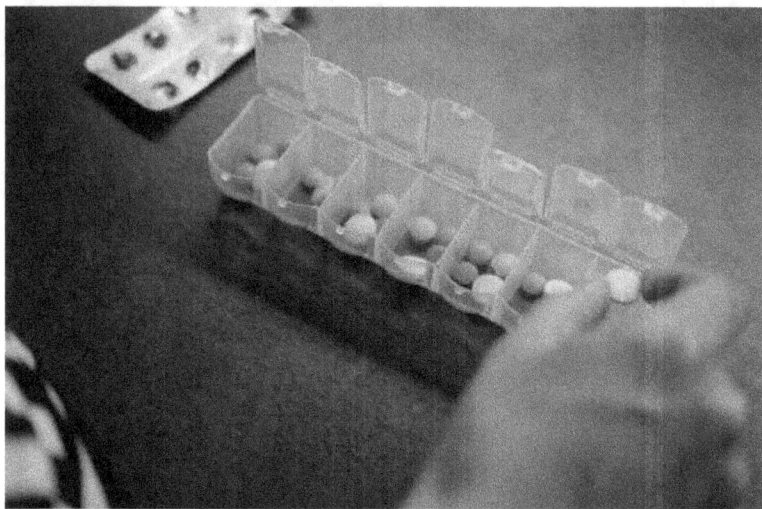

Key competencies for medical representatives form the foundation of success in the pharmaceutical industry. These competencies encompass a blend of specialized knowledge, interpersonal skills, and strategic thinking that empower representatives to effectively engage healthcare providers. A profound understanding of pharmaceutical products and therapeutic areas is crucial, as it enables representatives to communicate the benefits and risks of medications confidently. Mastery of product knowledge allows medical representatives to address healthcare professionals' queries and concerns, establishing credibility and trust.

Effective communication skills are indispensable for medical representatives. They must be able to convey complex medical information clearly and concisely, tailoring their approach to suit the audience's level of understanding. This includes not only verbal communication but also active listening skills, which are essential for identifying the specific needs and preferences of healthcare providers. Furthermore, the ability to present information persuasively can influence prescriber behavior and foster long-term relationships that are vital for sustained success.

Building effective relationships with healthcare providers is another key competency. This involves understanding the dynamics of the healthcare environment and recognizing the unique challenges that healthcare professionals face. Medical representatives should engage in meaningful conversations that go beyond sales pitches, showing genuine interest in providers' needs and concerns. Developing rapport and trust can lead to more productive interactions and encourage healthcare professionals to consider the representative's products seriously.

Navigating regulatory compliance is also critical for medical representatives. The pharmaceutical industry is heavily regulated, and representatives must be well-versed in the legal and ethical standards governing their interactions with healthcare providers. This knowledge not only ensures compliance but also enhances the representative's reputation and fosters confidence among healthcare professionals. Understanding the nuances of regulatory requirements can help representatives avoid pitfalls and maintain professional integrity.

Finally, leveraging data and analytics stands as a vital competency in today's data-driven environment. Medical representatives should be adept at utilizing market research, sales data, and performance metrics to inform their strategies and decision-making. This analytical approach enables representatives to identify trends, understand market access dynamics, and tailor their sales techniques effectively. Embracing digital marketing strategies also plays a crucial role in reaching healthcare providers in a more targeted and efficient manner, further enhancing the representative's ability to succeed in the competitive pharmaceutical landscape.

Setting Goals and Objectives for Success

Setting clear and actionable goals and objectives is a vital component of achieving success in the pharmaceutical industry. For sales and marketing representatives, as well as managers, having a structured approach to goal-setting can significantly enhance performance and drive results. Goals should be specific, measurable, achievable, relevant, and time-bound (SMART). This framework not only ensures clarity but also provides a roadmap for tracking progress and making necessary adjustments along the way. By establishing concrete objectives, professionals can maintain focus and motivation in a dynamic and competitive environment.

In the context of pharmaceutical sales, it is essential to align goals with the broader organizational strategy. Representatives should consider how their contributions can support the company's mission and vision. For instance, setting objectives related to building effective relationships with healthcare providers can lead to increased trust and collaboration, ultimately influencing prescription behaviors. Furthermore, aligning personal goals with those of the organization fosters a sense of ownership and accountability, encouraging representatives to actively participate in the company's success.

Achieving effective goal-setting necessitates a thorough understanding of the market environment. Sales representatives need to be knowledgeable about the therapeutic areas they represent and the regulatory guidelines that influence their work. Utilizing data and analytics enables them to pinpoint trends, opportunities, and challenges that shape their goals. For instance, by examining sales figures and market access approaches, representatives can establish achievable targets for product launches or promotional efforts, making sure their objectives are realistic and backed by data.

In addition, fostering a culture of continuous improvement through training and development programs is crucial for achieving long-term success. Organizations should prioritize equipping their sales teams with the skills necessary to navigate the complexities of pharmaceutical sales. This includes enhancing communication skills, mastering sales techniques, and understanding reimbursement strategies. By committing to ongoing professional development, representatives can adapt to changing market conditions and refine their approach to meet evolving customer needs.

Finally, it is important to regularly review and adjust goals and objectives as needed. The pharmaceutical landscape is constantly evolving, and what may have been a relevant target at one point may no longer apply. By establishing a regular cadence for reviewing progress, sales representatives and managers can ensure they remain agile and responsive to new challenges. This iterative process not only helps in achieving immediate objectives but also contributes to long-term career advancement opportunities in the pharmaceutical sales sector, allowing professionals to stay ahead in a competitive market.

Chapter 3: Building Effective Relationships with Healthcare Providers

Identifying Key Stakeholders

Identifying key stakeholders is an essential part of the pharmaceutical sales process. Stakeholders include a wide range of individuals and organizations that have an impact on or are impacted by the pharmaceutical product or service. For medical representatives, it is crucial to identify these stakeholders and comprehend their roles and viewpoints to establish strong relationships and manage the complexities of the healthcare landscape. This insight not only supports sales efforts but also improves the capability to convey the product's value effectively.

The primary stakeholders in the pharmaceutical landscape include healthcare providers, payers, patients, and regulatory bodies. Healthcare providers, such as physicians, pharmacists, and nurses, play a pivotal role in the decision-making process regarding which medications to prescribe or recommend. Building relationships with these professionals is crucial, as they are often the frontline influencers of pharmaceutical products. It is essential to understand their clinical needs, preferences, and concerns to tailor your approach effectively. Additionally, engaging with payers, who determine coverage and reimbursement policies, can significantly impact the market access of your products.

Patients are arguably the most important stakeholders in the pharmaceutical sector, as they are the end-users of the products. Understanding patient demographics, needs, and treatment experiences can help medical representatives communicate the benefits and relevance of their products more effectively. Engaging patients through educational initiatives and support programs can also foster loyalty and trust. Moreover, involving patient advocacy groups can enhance your outreach efforts, as these organizations can provide valuable insights into patient needs and preferences.

Regulatory bodies represent another crucial stakeholder group, as they establish the guidelines and standards that govern the pharmaceutical industry. Understanding the regulatory landscape is vital for medical representatives to ensure compliance and navigate potential challenges during the sales process. Familiarity with regulations can also enhance credibility when discussing product information with healthcare providers. Keeping abreast of changes in regulations, as well as understanding the approval processes for new drugs, can significantly influence strategic planning and stakeholder engagement.

Finally, leveraging data and analytics to identify and prioritize stakeholders can optimize your sales efforts. Analyzing market trends, healthcare provider behaviour, and patient demographics allows for a more targeted approach to stakeholder engagement. Additionally, utilizing digital marketing strategies can help reach a broader audience and facilitate communication with stakeholders. By effectively identifying and understanding key stakeholders, medical representatives can enhance their sales techniques, build lasting relationships, and contribute to the overall success of their pharmaceutical products in the market.

Establishing Trust and Credibility

Establishing trust and credibility is paramount for medical representatives navigating the complex pharmaceutical landscape. In an industry characterized by rigorous regulatory frameworks and heightened scrutiny, the ability to build authentic relationships with healthcare providers is essential. Trust serves as the foundation upon which effective communication and collaboration are built. When healthcare professionals perceive a representative as trustworthy, they are more likely to engage openly, share insights, and consider the products being presented. This relationship not only enhances sales opportunities but also contributes to better patient care through informed decision-making.

To foster trust, representatives should prioritize transparency in their interactions. This involves being upfront about product information, potential side effects, and any financial incentives that may be associated with their offerings. A commitment to honesty demonstrates integrity and respect for the healthcare provider's expertise and decision-making process. Moreover, keeping lines of communication open, addressing concerns promptly, and being receptive to feedback further solidifies credibility. In a landscape where information is abundant but often conflicting, a representative who consistently provides accurate and reliable information stands out as a valuable resource.

Developing therapeutic expertise is another critical component in establishing credibility. Medical representatives should invest time in understanding the products they represent and the therapeutic areas they operate in. This knowledge enables them to engage in meaningful discussions with healthcare providers, allowing for a deeper exploration of how their products can meet specific patient needs. When representatives can articulate the clinical benefits and nuances of their products, they position themselves as knowledgeable partners rather than mere salespeople. This expertise not only builds trust but also enhances the representative's confidence when addressing complex inquiries.

Utilizing data and analytics is instrumental in reinforcing trust and credibility as well. By leveraging market insights, representatives can tailor their conversations to align with the specific interests and challenges faced by healthcare providers. This data-driven approach demonstrates a commitment to understanding the provider's practice and the patient population they serve. Additionally, sharing relevant research findings or case studies can support the claims being made about the product, further enhancing the representative's credibility. The ability to back up assertions with evidence fosters a sense of reliability and professionalism.

Finally, ongoing training and development are essential for maintaining credibility over time. The pharmaceutical industry is constantly evolving, with new regulations, products, and market dynamics emerging regularly. Representatives and managers must prioritize continuous education to stay informed and adapt to these changes. This commitment to professional growth not only enriches the representative's knowledge base but also signals to healthcare providers that they are engaging with a dedicated professional. In doing so, representatives can cultivate long-lasting relationships built on trust, ultimately contributing to their success in the pharmaceutical field.

Networking Strategies for Success

Networking is a critical component of success in the pharmaceutical industry, particularly for sales and marketing representatives. Building a robust network not only enhances your visibility but also facilitates the exchange of valuable information and resources. Effective networking goes beyond merely attending industry events; it requires a strategic approach to cultivate meaningful relationships with healthcare providers, peers, and industry leaders. By identifying key stakeholders and engaging with them regularly, representatives can create a supportive ecosystem that fosters collaboration and knowledge sharing.

To maximize networking opportunities, it is essential to leverage both in-person and digital platforms. In-person events, such as conferences and seminars, offer unique opportunities to meet potential collaborators and clients face-to-face. However, the rise of digital communication tools has transformed networking dynamics, allowing representatives to connect with a broader audience through webinars, social media, and professional networking sites. By maintaining an active online presence, representatives can showcase their expertise, share industry insights, and engage with stakeholders in real-time, thereby enhancing their professional credibility.

Building effective relationships with healthcare providers is paramount for success in pharmaceutical sales. Understanding their needs, preferences, and challenges allows representatives to tailor their approaches and provide relevant solutions. Regular follow-ups and check-ins can reinforce these relationships, ensuring that representatives remain top-of-mind when healthcare providers require pharmaceutical products or services. Additionally, hosting educational sessions or workshops can position representatives as trusted advisors, further solidifying their connections with healthcare professionals.

Networking also plays a vital role in navigating regulatory compliance in the pharmaceutical industry. By connecting with compliance experts and legal advisors, sales representatives can gain insights into best practices and stay informed about changing regulations. This knowledge not only protects the organization but also empowers representatives to communicate confidently and ethically with healthcare providers. Establishing these connections can provide a safety net, ensuring that representatives are equipped to handle compliance-related challenges effectively.

Finally, continuous development through networking can open doors to career advancement opportunities within the pharmaceutical sector. Engaging in professional associations and industry groups provides access to mentorship, training programs, and resources that can enhance skill sets and knowledge. By actively participating in these networks, representatives can learn about emerging trends, market access strategies, and reimbursement models, positioning themselves as informed professionals ready to tackle the complexities of the pharmaceutical landscape. Ultimately, a well-cultivated network can be a powerful asset that drives success and growth in the competitive field of pharmaceutical sales.

Chapter 4: Mastering Pharmaceutical Sales Techniques

Consultative Selling Approaches

Consultative selling approaches have become essential for medical representatives in the pharmaceutical industry as they navigate complex healthcare environments. This method shifts the focus from merely selling products to understanding and addressing the specific needs of healthcare providers. By building a genuine rapport with physicians and their staff, representatives can better identify pain points and offer tailored solutions, thus fostering long-term relationships that benefit both parties.

This strategic approach not only enhances customer satisfaction but also positions the medical representative as a trusted advisor rather than just a salesperson.

In implementing consultative selling, representatives must develop robust product knowledge and therapeutic expertise. This knowledge allows them to engage healthcare providers in meaningful conversations about treatment options and patient outcomes. By demonstrating a deep understanding of their products and relevant therapeutic areas, representatives can effectively communicate how their offerings align with the healthcare provider's goals. This level of expertise also empowers representatives to address potential objections with confidence, further solidifying their role as knowledgeable partners in patient care.

Effective communication skills are a cornerstone of consultative selling. Medical representatives must be adept at active listening, ensuring they fully understand the concerns and needs of healthcare providers. By asking insightful questions and genuinely engaging in dialogue, representatives can uncover underlying issues that may not be immediately apparent. This approach not only helps in identifying suitable solutions but also fosters trust and collaboration. Furthermore, honing communication skills involves not just verbal interactions but also the ability to articulate complex information clearly and concisely, which is vital in the fast-paced pharmaceutical environment.

Leveraging data and analytics is another critical component of consultative selling in the pharmaceutical sector. Sales representatives can utilize analytics to gain insights into market trends, provider behaviour, and patient outcomes. This data-driven approach enables representatives to tailor their messaging and strategies to align with the specific needs of healthcare providers. By presenting relevant data during conversations, representatives can reinforce their recommendations and demonstrate the value of their products tangibly. This not only enhances the credibility of the representative but also supports informed decision-making among healthcare providers.

Finally, training and development programs play an essential role in equipping medical representatives with the skills necessary for successful consultative selling. Organizations should invest in ongoing training that focuses on enhancing communication skills, product knowledge, and the effective use of data analytics. These programs not only prepare representatives for the challenges they will face in the field but also promote a culture of continuous improvement and professional growth. As representatives advance their skills and knowledge, they will be better positioned to engage healthcare providers in meaningful ways, ultimately driving success in the competitive pharmaceutical landscape.

Overcoming Objections and Rejections

Overcoming objections and rejections is a critical skill for any medical representative in the pharmaceutical industry. While encountering resistance is an inevitable part of the sales process, how you handle these challenges can significantly impact your success and relationships with healthcare providers. To build trust and credibility, representatives must first understand the common objections that arise during their interactions. These objections may stem from concerns about the product, the perceived value, or previous experiences with pharmaceutical companies. By recognizing these barriers, representatives can prepare effective responses that address the healthcare provider's specific concerns, fostering a constructive dialogue.

One effective strategy for overcoming objections is to actively listen to the healthcare provider's concerns without interrupting. This demonstrates respect and allows you to gain valuable insights into their perspective. When you fully understand their objections, you can tailor your response to directly address their specific issues. For instance, if a provider is skeptical about the efficacy of a new medication, sharing relevant clinical trial data, testimonials from peers, or comparative studies can help alleviate their concerns. Incorporating evidence-based information not only builds credibility but also reinforces the value of the product being presented.

In addition to addressing objections, it is essential to reframe rejection as an opportunity for growth rather than a setback. Every "no" can provide insights into improving your approach or understanding the market better. After a rejection, take the time to reflect on the interaction. Consider asking open-ended questions to the healthcare provider about their reasons for declining. This feedback can be instrumental in refining your pitch and enhancing your overall effectiveness. Moreover, maintaining a positive attitude in the face of rejection is crucial. A resilient mindset enables representatives to persist and adapt their strategies, ultimately leading to greater success.

Building effective relationships with healthcare providers is also pivotal in overcoming objections and rejections. Establishing rapport can create an environment where providers feel comfortable voicing their concerns and can lead to more open communication. Regularly engaging with healthcare professionals through follow-up visits, informative emails, or educational workshops can strengthen these connections. By positioning yourself as a reliable resource and partner in their practice, you increase the likelihood of them considering your products in the future, even after initial objections.

Lastly, ongoing training and development are vital for mastering the art of overcoming objections and rejections. Participating in workshops, role-playing scenarios, and peer feedback sessions can enhance your skills and build your confidence. Familiarity with various sales techniques and objection-handling strategies will prepare representatives to navigate challenging conversations effectively. Regularly updating your product knowledge and understanding market dynamics will also empower you to address objections with authority. Ultimately, embracing the journey of overcoming objections will not only improve your sales performance but will also foster a culture of resilience and adaptability within your team, driving the pharmaceutical industry's success.

Closing Techniques for Sales Success

Closing techniques are crucial in the pharmaceutical sales process, ensuring that representatives effectively convert leads into loyal customers. A well-timed and strategically executed closing technique can make the difference between a successful sale and a missed opportunity. Understanding the nuances of these techniques is essential for sales and marketing representatives as they navigate complex relationships with healthcare providers and decision-makers. Building a rapport throughout the sales process leads to a more natural transition into closing, where representatives can confidently address any lingering objections and guide the conversation toward a decision.

One effective closing technique is the assumptive close, where the representative proceeds under the assumption that the prospect is ready to make a purchase. This approach allows the sales representative to maintain a confident demeanour while discussing the next steps, such as scheduling a delivery or discussing payment options. By framing the conversation in this manner, representatives can reinforce the idea that the decision to buy has already been made. This technique can be particularly effective in the pharmaceutical industry, where healthcare providers appreciate efficiency and clarity in the decision-making process.

Another powerful technique is the urgency close, which creates a sense of time sensitivity around the purchase decision. In pharmaceutical sales, this can be framed around limited-time offers or the potential benefits of early adoption of a new drug or therapy. By highlighting the advantages of acting quickly, representatives can motivate healthcare providers to make decisions more swiftly. However, it is essential to use this technique ethically, ensuring that the urgency is genuine and based on real benefits rather than pressure tactics.

The consultative close is another approach that emphasizes the representative's role as a trusted advisor. In this technique, representatives engage healthcare providers in a discussion about their needs and concerns, positioning themselves as partners in finding the best solutions for patient care. By aligning the product benefits with the provider's goals, representatives can create a compelling case for why the provider should choose their product. This technique requires a deep understanding of both the product and the therapeutic area, as well as strong communication skills to effectively convey this alignment.

Finally, the follow-up close is an essential technique in pharmaceutical sales. After initial meetings or presentations, representatives should establish a systematic follow-up routine to maintain engagement and address any further questions or concerns. This technique not only reinforces the representative's commitment to the healthcare provider but also keeps the conversation alive, increasing the chances of closing the sale. By utilizing various closing techniques tailored to specific situations and relationships, pharmaceutical sales representatives can enhance their effectiveness and drive success in their roles.

Chapter 5: Navigating Regulatory Compliance in Pharma

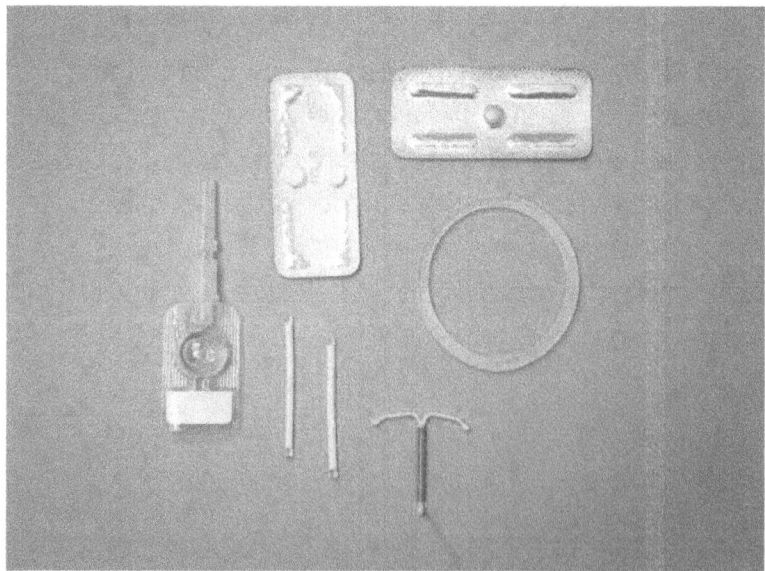

Understanding Regulatory Frameworks

Understanding regulatory frameworks is crucial for sales and marketing representatives and managers in the pharmaceutical industry. These frameworks encompass the rules, guidelines, and laws that govern the development, approval, marketing, and distribution of pharmaceutical products. A comprehensive understanding of these regulations not only ensures compliance but also facilitates effective communication with healthcare providers and enhances the credibility of representatives. Regulatory bodies, such as the Food and Drug Administration (FDA) in the United States or the European Medicines Agency (EMA) in Europe, play a pivotal role in establishing these standards, which are designed to protect patient safety and promote public health.

The regulatory environment is intricate and continuously changing, making it crucial for pharmaceutical professionals to remain updated. This means grasping the different phases of drug development, ranging from preclinical trials to post-marketing surveillance. Each phase is subject to particular regulations that outline how products must be tested, approved, and monitored. For example, securing marketing authorization necessitates comprehensive documentation of clinical trial outcomes, manufacturing procedures, and labelling details. Failing to meet these requirements can result in delays or denials, negatively impacting market access and sales opportunities.

Moreover, regulatory frameworks also impact promotional activities and communication strategies. Pharmaceutical representatives must be well-versed in the guidelines that dictate how they can engage with healthcare providers, share information about products, and promote their benefits. Missteps in this area can lead to significant legal repercussions, including fines and damage to the company's reputation. Understanding the boundaries of acceptable promotion helps representatives build trust with healthcare professionals and fosters long-term relationships that are essential for success in the field.

In addition to direct regulatory compliance, representatives should also be aware of the broader implications of these frameworks on market access and reimbursement strategies. Payers often rely on regulatory approvals to determine coverage and reimbursement for pharmaceutical products. A deep understanding of how regulatory decisions influence these aspects can empower sales and marketing teams to craft more effective strategies. By aligning their promotional efforts with regulatory expectations, representatives can better position their products in the marketplace, enhancing their chances of success.

Lastly, continuous education and training on regulatory matters are vital for all professionals in the pharmaceutical industry. Engaging in ongoing learning opportunities, such as workshops, seminars, and online courses, can help ensure that representatives and managers are up to date with the latest regulations and best practices. This commitment to compliance not only safeguards the organization's reputation but also contributes to the overall integrity of the pharmaceutical industry. By prioritizing regulatory understanding, pharmaceutical professionals can navigate the complexities of the market and drive their success in a competitive environment.

The Importance of Compliance in Pharmaceutical Sales

The importance of compliance in pharmaceutical sales cannot be overstated, as it serves as the foundation for the integrity and trustworthiness of the industry. Compliance refers to the adherence to laws, regulations, and ethical standards that govern the promotion and sale of pharmaceutical products. For sales and marketing representatives, understanding compliance is essential not only to avoid legal repercussions but also to foster strong, long-lasting relationships with healthcare providers. These relationships are built on trust, and any breach of compliance can damage reputations and erode confidence among healthcare professionals.

Understanding regulatory compliance is essential in an industry that faces significant oversight from government agencies and industry groups. The pharmaceutical sector is filled with regulations concerning advertising, promotional activities, and sample distribution. Sales representatives need to be knowledgeable about these rules to ensure their marketing approaches meet legal standards. This understanding not only reduces the likelihood of penalties but also enables representatives to conduct ethical marketing that focuses on patient welfare and the responsible promotion of medications.

Furthermore, compliance plays a key role in maintaining the pharmaceutical industry's reputation. When companies prioritize compliance, they signal to the public and healthcare professionals that they are committed to ethical standards and patient safety. This commitment can enhance a company's brand image and facilitate smoother interactions with healthcare providers. In a highly competitive market, a strong reputation can be a significant differentiator, making compliance an integral aspect of any sales strategy.

In addition to legal and ethical considerations, compliance also intersects with effective communication strategies. Medical representatives must communicate product information accurately and transparently, ensuring that healthcare providers have the necessary information to make informed decisions for their patients. This requires not only a thorough understanding of the products being sold but also an awareness of the regulatory framework that governs how this information can be presented. By mastering compliant communication, representatives can build credibility and trust with healthcare providers, ultimately leading to better sales outcomes.

Finally, the integration of compliance into the training and development programs for sales representatives is vital. Ongoing education about regulatory changes and ethical considerations should be a core component of any training initiative. By equipping representatives with the knowledge and tools they need to navigate compliance issues, organizations can foster a culture of accountability and ethical behavior. A well-informed sales force not only protects the organization from potential violations but also enhances the overall effectiveness of sales efforts, creating a pathway to sustainable success in the pharmaceutical industry.

Best Practices for Navigating Regulations

Navigating the regulations in the pharmaceutical sector is essential for maintaining compliance and successfully promoting products. Sales and marketing representatives need to have a solid grasp of the legal and ethical standards that guide their actions. This knowledge safeguards the organization against potential legal issues and fosters trust with healthcare providers and patients. A robust foundation in regulatory compliance starts with thorough training programs that emphasize the necessity of staying updated on industry regulations, including those established by the Food and Drug Administration (FDA) and other regulatory authorities.

One of the best practices for navigating regulations is to cultivate a culture of transparency within the organization. Encouraging open discussions about regulatory changes and their implications fosters an environment where sales representatives feel empowered to seek guidance when uncertain about compliance matters. Regularly scheduled training sessions, workshops, and updates on regulatory news can help ensure that all team members are on the same page. This proactive approach not only minimizes the risk of violations but also enhances the credibility of the sales force when interacting with healthcare providers.

Another essential practice is to develop and maintain strong relationships with compliance and legal teams. Sales representatives should not hesitate to engage these departments when questions about marketing materials or promotional strategies arise. By collaborating closely with compliance specialists, representatives can ensure that their initiatives align with current regulations, which ultimately leads to more effective and compliant marketing campaigns. This partnership also provides an avenue for representatives to gain insights into how regulations are evolving, enabling them to adapt their strategies accordingly.

Utilizing digital tools and resources can significantly aid in navigating regulatory compliance. Online databases and platforms that track regulatory changes allow representatives to stay informed about new guidelines and requirements. Additionally, leveraging data analytics can help identify trends in compliance issues and assess the effectiveness of current strategies. By integrating technology into their daily routines, sales and marketing representatives can enhance their ability to respond swiftly to regulatory shifts, ensuring their practices remain compliant.

Lastly, fostering a commitment to ethical practices is paramount. Sales and marketing representatives should always prioritize the well-being of patients and healthcare providers over sales goals. By adhering to ethical standards and advocating for responsible marketing practices, representatives can contribute to a positive industry reputation. This commitment not only helps in avoiding regulatory pitfalls but also strengthens relationships with stakeholders, positioning representatives as trusted partners in the healthcare ecosystem. Emphasizing ethics in every aspect of pharmaceutical sales and marketing is an indispensable element for long-term success in navigating regulatory landscapes.

Chapter 6: Utilizing Digital Marketing Strategies for Pharma Sales

Overview of Digital Marketing in Pharma

Digital marketing has transformed the pharmaceutical industry, offering innovative ways for companies to engage with healthcare providers and patients. In an era where digital interactions are paramount, pharmaceutical sales and marketing representatives must adapt to new strategies that leverage online platforms and tools. This subchapter provides an overview of how digital marketing is reshaping the landscape of pharmaceutical sales, emphasizing its importance for relationship building, compliance, and overall market success.

The growth of digital marketing in the pharmaceutical sector is fueled by the demand for more precise communication. Conventional marketing methods frequently fall short of effectively reaching particular healthcare professionals. Digital platforms like social media, email marketing, and dedicated healthcare websites enable representatives to customize their messages according to the specific needs and preferences of their audience. This tailored approach not only boosts engagement but also builds stronger connections with healthcare providers by providing pertinent information that supports their clinical decision-making.

Moreover, the integration of data analytics into digital marketing strategies enhances the ability of pharmaceutical companies to track and measure the effectiveness of their campaigns. By analyzing metrics such as engagement rates, conversion rates, and audience feedback, sales representatives can gain valuable insights into what resonates with healthcare providers and adjust their approaches accordingly. This data-driven methodology empowers representatives to make informed decisions, ensuring that their marketing efforts are both efficient and impactful in a highly competitive environment.

Regulatory compliance remains a critical consideration in digital marketing within the pharmaceutical sector. The industry is subject to stringent guidelines regarding advertising and promotion, particularly in how products are presented to healthcare providers. Understanding these regulations is essential for sales representatives to navigate the complex landscape without risking compliance violations. Digital marketing strategies must therefore be designed with these guidelines in mind, ensuring that all communications are not only effective but also adhere to legal and ethical standards.

Finally, as digital marketing continues to evolve, it presents ongoing opportunities for professional development within the pharmaceutical sales field. Representatives who embrace these changes can enhance their skills in digital communication, data interpretation, and relationship management. Continuous training in digital marketing strategies will not only improve individual performance but also contribute to the overall success of the pharmaceutical organization. By investing in their digital acumen, sales and marketing professionals can better position themselves for career advancement while driving their companies toward greater market success.

Social Media Strategies for Engagement

Social media has emerged as a powerful tool for pharmaceutical companies seeking to engage healthcare professionals and patients alike. A well-structured social media strategy can enhance brand visibility, foster relationships, and facilitate the sharing of critical information. For sales and marketing representatives in the pharmaceutical industry, understanding the nuances of social media engagement is essential. This begins with identifying the right platforms where target audiences congregate. LinkedIn, for example, is invaluable for connecting with healthcare providers and industry peers, while Twitter can be effective for real-time updates and discussions on industry trends and developments.

Creating compelling content is another critical aspect of social media engagement. Representatives must focus on delivering value through educational posts, infographics, and videos that highlight product benefits, therapeutic areas, and patient success stories. Engaging content not only captures attention but also encourages shares and discussions, extending the reach of the message. Regularly updating content and maintaining an active presence on social media platforms can position representatives as thought leaders in their respective fields, fostering trust and credibility among healthcare providers.

Interaction is a cornerstone of effective social media strategies. Engaging with followers through comments, direct messages, and responding to inquiries can significantly enhance relationships. Representatives should aim to initiate conversations, ask for feedback, and create polls or surveys to better understand the needs and preferences of their audience. This two-way communication builds a community around the brand, making healthcare providers feel valued and more likely to engage with the brand on a deeper level.

Compliance with regulatory guidelines is paramount in the pharmaceutical industry, especially within the realm of social media. Representatives must ensure that all content adheres to the legal frameworks governing pharmaceutical advertising and communication. This includes being transparent about product information, avoiding misleading claims, and ensuring that any interactions with healthcare professionals comply with ethical standards. Training on regulatory compliance should be an integral part of any social media strategy to mitigate risks associated with non-compliance.

Finally, measuring the effectiveness of social media engagement strategies is essential for continuous improvement. Utilizing data analytics tools can provide insights into audience engagement levels, content performance, and overall reach. Sales and marketing representatives should regularly assess these metrics to refine their strategies, ensuring that they align with the evolving needs of healthcare providers and patients. By embracing a data-driven approach, representatives can optimize their social media efforts, ultimately contributing to their success in the pharmaceutical industry.

Leveraging Content Marketing for Product Promotion

In the contemporary pharmaceutical landscape, leveraging content marketing for product promotion is becoming increasingly essential for sales and marketing representatives. Content marketing provides a strategic approach to engaging healthcare professionals and patients, offering valuable information that fosters trust and credibility. By creating high-quality content that educates and informs, representatives can position themselves as knowledgeable resources, ultimately leading to stronger relationships with healthcare providers. This method transcends traditional promotional tactics, allowing for a more nuanced and effective way to communicate the benefits of pharmaceutical products.

Effective content marketing begins with a clear understanding of the target audience. For pharmaceutical representatives, this means identifying the specific needs and interests of healthcare providers and patients. By conducting thorough market research and utilizing data analytics, representatives can tailor their content to address the unique challenges faced by their audience. This targeted approach not only enhances engagement but also ensures that the content resonates with the audience, making it more likely to influence their perceptions and decisions regarding a product.

Incorporating various content formats can further enhance the effectiveness of marketing efforts. Written articles, infographics, videos, and webinars can all play a role in engagingly delivering information. For instance, a well-researched white paper discussing the latest clinical developments in a therapeutic area can provide healthcare providers with valuable insights, thereby establishing the representative as a credible source of information. Additionally, utilizing digital platforms to disseminate this content ensures that it reaches a wider audience, maximizing the potential for engagement and interaction.

Moreover, integrating content marketing with social media strategies can amplify outreach efforts. Social media platforms allow pharmaceutical representatives to share their content, engage in discussions, and respond to inquiries in real-time. This interaction not only builds relationships but also creates a community around the brand, encouraging healthcare providers to share their experiences and insights. By actively participating in these conversations, representatives can further reinforce their authority and commitment to supporting healthcare professionals.

Lastly, measuring the effectiveness of content marketing initiatives is crucial for continuous improvement. By leveraging analytics tools, representatives can track engagement metrics, such as website traffic, content shares, and audience feedback. This data provides invaluable insights into what resonates with the audience and what may require adjustment. By consistently evaluating and refining their content marketing strategies, pharmaceutical representatives can enhance their promotional efforts, ensuring that they remain relevant and impactful in the evolving healthcare landscape.

Chapter 7: Developing Product Knowledge and Therapeutic Expertise

Importance of In-Depth Product Knowledge

In the competitive landscape of the pharmaceutical industry, in-depth product knowledge emerges as a cornerstone for success. For sales and marketing representatives, possessing a comprehensive understanding of the products they promote not only enhances their credibility but also enables them to effectively communicate the clinical benefits and unique selling propositions to healthcare providers.

This knowledge is crucial in navigating discussions around therapeutic areas, patient outcomes, and treatment protocols, ultimately fostering trust and building lasting relationships with healthcare professionals.

Furthermore, detailed product knowledge empowers representatives to address potential objections and questions from healthcare providers. When representatives can articulate the scientific rationale behind a product, including its mechanism of action, safety profile, and comparative effectiveness, they position themselves as valuable resources. This not only aids in overcoming reservations but also demonstrates a commitment to patient care, aligning the representative's goals with those of healthcare providers who prioritize patient outcomes.

In addition, mastering product knowledge facilitates more strategic sales techniques. Representatives equipped with insights about market trends, competitor products, and evolving therapeutic guidelines can tailor their sales pitches more effectively. By understanding the specific needs of their audience, they can engage in meaningful conversations that resonate with healthcare providers' experiences and challenges.

This approach not only enhances the likelihood of a successful sale but also positions the representative as a knowledgeable partner in the treatment journey.

Moreover, in-depth product knowledge plays a vital role in compliance with regulatory standards. The pharmaceutical industry is heavily regulated, and representatives must navigate complex legal landscapes while promoting their products. A thorough understanding of product specifications, indications, contraindications, and safety information ensures that representatives communicate responsibly and ethically. This adherence to compliance not only protects the organization from potential legal repercussions but also reinforces the integrity of the representative in the eyes of healthcare providers.

Lastly, continuous learning and development in product knowledge are essential for career advancement within the pharmaceutical sector. Representatives who commit to ongoing education about their products and therapeutic areas are better positioned for leadership roles. By demonstrating expertise and a proactive approach to learning, these individuals can establish themselves as industry leaders, paving the way for future opportunities in sales management or specialized roles within the pharmaceutical field. This commitment to knowledge not only benefits the individual but also contributes to the overall success and reputation of the organization.

Therapeutic Areas and their Relevance

Therapeutic areas play a crucial role in the pharmaceutical industry, directly impacting the strategies employed by sales representatives and managers. Understanding these areas is essential for medical representatives as they navigate the complexities of their roles. Each therapeutic area encompasses specific diseases and conditions, which require distinct treatment approaches and product knowledge.

By familiarizing themselves with these areas, representatives can tailor their sales techniques and communication to meet the unique needs of healthcare providers, ultimately fostering stronger relationships and improving patient outcomes.

The relevance of therapeutic areas extends beyond mere product knowledge; it influences market access and reimbursement strategies as well. Different therapeutic areas face varying levels of scrutiny and regulation, which can affect how products are positioned and accessed within the healthcare system. Medical representatives must grasp the nuances of these areas to effectively communicate the value of their products to healthcare providers and payers. This understanding helps in anticipating challenges related to reimbursement processes, allowing representatives to present comprehensive solutions that align with both clinical needs and economic considerations.

The therapeutic landscape is continually changing due to progress in medical research and shifts in patient demographics. This ever-evolving environment requires sales and marketing representatives to keep updated on new trends and treatment options in their specific therapeutic areas. By remaining informed, they can discover fresh opportunities to engage with healthcare providers and adjust their sales strategies as needed. Ongoing education and training in therapeutic knowledge equip representatives to act as trusted advisors, boosting their credibility and strengthening their relationships with their audience.

Digital marketing strategies have also become integral to navigating therapeutic areas effectively. As healthcare providers increasingly rely on digital resources for information, representatives must leverage these platforms to disseminate relevant product knowledge and therapeutic insights. Utilizing data analytics can enhance understanding of market trends and provider preferences, allowing representatives to craft targeted communications that resonate with their audience. This strategic approach not only boosts sales performance but also aligns with the broader shift toward personalized medicine and patient-centere care.

In conclusion, the significance of therapeutic areas in pharmaceutical sales cannot be overstated. For sales and marketing representatives, a deep understanding of these areas is essential for building effective relationships with healthcare providers, mastering sales techniques, and navigating the complexities of market access. By committing to ongoing education and utilizing digital tools, representatives can enhance their expertise and adaptability in an ever-changing landscape. Ultimately, this knowledge translates into improved sales outcomes and contributes to the overall success of the pharmaceutical industry.

Continuous Learning and Staying Updated

Continuous learning is a cornerstone of professional success in the pharmaceutical industry, particularly for sales and marketing representatives. The rapid pace of advancements in medical science, evolving regulations, and changing market dynamics necessitate an ongoing commitment to education. By staying informed about the latest pharmaceutical developments, representatives can enhance their product knowledge and therapeutic expertise, which directly contributes to their ability to build effective relationships with healthcare providers. This commitment to continuous learning not only empowers representatives but also reinforces the credibility and trust required to engage with healthcare professionals.

To effectively navigate the complexities of the pharmaceutical landscape, representatives must actively seek opportunities for training and development. This can include formal education programs, workshops, webinars, and industry conferences that focus on critical topics such as regulatory compliance, market access strategies, and emerging digital marketing techniques. Engaging in these educational initiatives allows representatives to enhance their skill sets and adapt to the ever-changing environment of pharmaceutical sales.

Furthermore, such training often provides insights into best practices and innovative approaches that can be applied to increase sales effectiveness.

In addition to structured learning, representatives should cultivate a habit of self-directed learning through resources such as industry publications, online courses, and professional networks. Leveraging platforms that offer updates on regulatory changes, clinical trial results, and market trends is essential for keeping pace with the industry. Moreover, utilizing data and analytics can help representatives identify customer needs and preferences, enabling them to tailor their approach and improve their communication skills.

This proactive approach to learning not only increases individual competence but also enhances the overall performance of the sales team.

Networking with peers and industry experts can also serve as an invaluable resource for continuous learning. Engaging in discussions with colleagues and mentors allows representatives to share experiences, insights, and strategies that have proven successful in their respective roles. These interactions can lead to new ideas and perspectives on tackling challenges in the field, ultimately fostering a culture of collaboration and support within the pharmaceutical sales community. In a sector that is increasingly reliant on innovation, the ability to adapt and learn from one another is a significant advantage.

Finally, organizations must prioritize continuous learning as part of their corporate culture. By investing in training and development programs for medical representatives, companies can ensure their teams are equipped with the knowledge and skills necessary to excel in their roles. Encouraging employees to pursue ongoing education not only enhances individual performance but also contributes to the overall success of the organization. In a competitive environment where staying updated is crucial, fostering a learning-oriented culture will empower representatives to navigate challenges effectively and drive pharmaceutical success.

Chapter 8: Enhancing Communication Skills for Medical Representatives

Verbal and Non-Verbal Communication Skills

Effective communication is a cornerstone of success in the pharmaceutical industry, especially for medical representatives who routinely engage with healthcare providers. Mastering both verbal and non-verbal communication skills can significantly enhance relationship-building efforts and ultimately drive sales. Verbal communication encompasses the words we choose and how we articulate our message, while non-verbal communication includes body language, facial expressions, and tone of voice. Together, these elements create a comprehensive communication strategy that can influence healthcare professionals' perceptions and decisions.

Verbal communication skills are crucial for conveying complex medical information clearly and persuasively. Medical representatives must be adept at tailoring their messages to meet the specific needs of their audience, whether they are speaking to a physician, pharmacist, or nurse. This involves not only understanding the product and its benefits but also actively listening to the concerns and questions of healthcare providers. Engaging in meaningful dialogue helps build trust and rapport, which are essential for fostering long-term professional relationships. Additionally, employing persuasive techniques such as storytelling can effectively illustrate the impact of a product, making the information more relatable and memorable.

Non-verbal communication plays a vital role in how messages are received. Research shows that a significant portion of communication is conveyed through body language, which can either reinforce or contradict spoken words. For medical representatives, maintaining eye contact, using open gestures, and displaying a confident posture can enhance their credibility and approachability. Furthermore, being attuned to the non-verbal cues of healthcare providers, such as their body language and facial expressions, can provide valuable insights into their level of interest and receptivity. This awareness allows representatives to adjust their approach in real time, fostering a more engaging and responsive dialogue.

In addition to face-to-face interactions, digital communication has become increasingly important in the pharmaceutical sector. With the rise of telemedicine and virtual meetings, representatives must adapt their communication strategies to effectively engage healthcare providers in a digital environment. This includes being proficient in using virtual meeting tools and understanding best practices for online presentations. Clear and concise language remains essential, but representatives must also be mindful of their virtual presence, ensuring that their non-verbal cues, such as facial expressions and gestures, translate well in a digital format.

Finally, training and development programs focused on enhancing communication skills should be a priority for pharmaceutical companies. Workshops that emphasize both verbal and non-verbal communication techniques can equip sales and marketing representatives with the tools necessary to excel in their roles. Role-playing scenarios and real-time feedback are effective methods for honing these skills, allowing representatives to practice and refine their approaches in a supportive environment. By investing in communication training, companies not only improve the capabilities of their representatives but also contribute to the overall success of their sales strategies within an increasingly competitive market.

Active Listening Techniques

Active listening is a vital skill for sales and marketing representatives in the pharmaceutical industry, as it fosters strong relationships with healthcare providers and enhances communication effectiveness. This technique goes beyond simply hearing words; it involves fully engaging with the speaker, demonstrating genuine interest, and responding appropriately. For medical representatives, mastering active listening can lead to a better understanding of healthcare providers' needs and concerns, ultimately driving successful sales outcomes.

One of the key components of active listening is paying attention to both verbal and non-verbal cues. This means not only focusing on the words being spoken but also observing body language, facial expressions, and tone of voice. For pharma representatives, this holistic approach allows for a more nuanced understanding of the provider's perspective. When a representative recognizes when a healthcare provider feels uncertain or enthusiastic, they can tailor their responses and strategies accordingly, thereby enhancing the effectiveness of their communication.

Another critical technique is reflecting and paraphrasing. By summarizing what the healthcare provider has said, representatives can confirm their understanding and show that they value the speaker's input. This technique not only clarifies any potential miscommunications but also encourages the provider to share more information. For instance, if a medical representative hears a provider express concerns about a particular treatment option, reflecting that concern helps to establish trust and openness, paving the way for a more productive dialogue.

Asking open-ended questions is another essential active listening technique that encourages deeper conversation. Instead of leading the provider toward a specific answer, open-ended questions invite them to express their thoughts and feelings more freely. This approach not only uncovers valuable insights into their preferences and experiences but also positions the representative as a consultative partner rather than just a salesperson. By fostering an environment of open communication, representatives can better align their offerings with the needs of healthcare providers.

Lastly, demonstrating empathy plays a crucial role in active listening. By acknowledging the emotions and challenges faced by healthcare providers, representatives can build rapport and strengthen relationships. Empathy involves not only understanding the provider's point of view but also validating their feelings and experiences. This connection can lead to increased loyalty and trust, making healthcare providers more receptive to discussing pharmaceutical products and services. In the competitive landscape of the pharmaceutical industry, employing active listening techniques can significantly enhance the effectiveness of medical representatives, ultimately contributing to their success and the success of their organizations.

Tailoring Communication to Different Audiences

Tailoring communication to different audiences is an essential skill for pharmaceutical sales and marketing representatives. Understanding the unique needs, preferences, and motivations of various stakeholders in the healthcare ecosystem enables representatives to deliver their messages more effectively. Whether engaging with healthcare providers, patients, or internal teams, adapting communication styles ensures clarity, fosters trust, and ultimately drives successful interactions. This approach not only enhances relationship-building efforts but also aligns with the overarching goal of improving patient outcomes.

For healthcare providers, the communication strategy should focus on evidence-based data, clinical efficacy, and therapeutic benefits of products. Medical representatives must be well-versed in the scientific aspects of their offerings, as healthcare professionals are often looking for in-depth knowledge to inform their treatment decisions. Presenting data clearly and compellingly, such as through case studies or clinical trial results, can substantiate claims and build credibility. Additionally, understanding the specific challenges faced by providers can help representatives tailor their discussions to offer relevant solutions, thereby reinforcing their role as trusted partners in patient care.

Conversely, when communicating with patients, the approach should be more empathetic and focused on understanding patient concerns and experiences. Simplifying complex medical jargon into relatable language is crucial, as patients may feel overwhelmed by medical terminology. Effective communication with patients involves not just conveying information about products but also actively listening to their needs and preferences. By establishing rapport and demonstrating genuine care, representatives can empower patients to make informed decisions about their health, thereby enhancing their overall experience with the pharmaceutical brand.

Internal communication within pharmaceutical organizations also requires a tailored approach. Sales and marketing managers must recognize the diverse backgrounds and expertise of their teams. Providing training sessions that address specific skill gaps while promoting a culture of open dialogue can enhance team collaboration and innovation.

Clear communication of company goals, product updates, and market trends will keep representatives informed and motivated, fostering a cohesive team environment that is essential for achieving sales targets. Furthermore, leveraging data analytics to share insights can enable more effective decision-making processes, ultimately driving performance.

Lastly, the digital landscape has transformed how pharmaceutical representatives communicate with various audiences. Utilizing digital marketing strategies allows for personalized outreach, enabling representatives to segment their audiences and tailor messages accordingly. Engaging content, such as webinars, social media, and email campaigns, can effectively reach healthcare providers and patients alike, providing valuable information in a convenient format. By embracing digital tools, representatives can enhance their communication strategies, ensuring that they remain relevant and responsive to the evolving needs of their audiences in an increasingly competitive marketplace.

Chapter 9: Leveraging Data and Analytics in Pharmaceutical Sales

Importance of Data-Driven Decision Making

Data-driven decision-making is essential in the pharmaceutical industry, particularly for sales and marketing representatives and managers. The landscape of healthcare is increasingly complex, with vast amounts of data generated daily from clinical trials, patient interactions, and market trends. By leveraging this data, professionals can make informed decisions that enhance their strategies and improve outcomes.

Understanding how to analyze and interpret data effectively allows representatives to identify opportunities, anticipate challenges, and respond proactively to market dynamics.

In the realm of pharmaceutical sales, data is not merely a collection of numbers; it is a valuable resource that can guide representatives in tailoring their approaches to healthcare providers. By utilizing data analytics, representatives can segment their target audience more effectively, ensuring that they engage with healthcare professionals using the most relevant information and solutions. This targeted approach fosters stronger relationships, as representatives can demonstrate an understanding of the specific needs and preferences of their clients, leading to enhanced trust and credibility.

Moreover, data-driven decision-making plays a crucial role in mastering pharmaceutical sales techniques. Sales representatives can analyze historical sales data to identify trends and patterns that inform their sales pitches. By understanding which products resonate best with specific demographics, representatives can customize their messaging and focus their efforts on the most promising leads. This strategic approach not only increases efficiency but also maximizes the potential for closing sales, ultimately contributing to the success of the organization.

Navigating regulatory compliance in the pharmaceutical industry is another area where data-driven insights are invaluable. The industry is subject to strict regulations, and staying compliant is essential for maintaining the integrity of operations. By harnessing data, representatives can track compliance metrics, identify potential areas of risk, and ensure that their practices align with regulatory standards. This proactive management of compliance not only mitigates risks but also reinforces the organization's reputation among healthcare providers and regulators alike.

Finally, utilizing digital marketing strategies in conjunction with data analytics opens new avenues for reaching healthcare providers effectively. Data can inform targeted digital campaigns, allowing representatives to engage with providers through channels that are most effective for their audience. By analyzing engagement metrics and adjusting strategies accordingly, representatives can enhance their outreach efforts, fostering greater brand awareness and product understanding. As the pharmaceutical landscape continues to evolve, embracing data-driven decision-making will be crucial for achieving sustained success in sales and marketing efforts.

Tools and Technologies for Data Analysis

Data analysis is an integral component of success in the pharmaceutical industry, particularly for sales and marketing representatives. Various tools and technologies are available that can significantly enhance the ability to interpret data, derive actionable insights, and make informed decisions. These tools range from basic spreadsheet applications to advanced analytics platforms. Understanding and effectively utilizing these technologies can empower representatives to better understand market trends, customer preferences, and the competitive landscape.

One of the most commonly used tools for data analysis in the pharmaceutical sector is Microsoft Excel. Excel offers a user-friendly interface for organizing data, performing calculations, and generating basic visualizations. While it may not provide the advanced analytics capabilities of more specialized software, its accessibility makes it a valuable tool for representatives who need to quickly analyze sales data, track performance metrics, or create reports. Learning to leverage Excel's features, such as pivot tables and graphs, can provide immediate benefits in understanding sales trends and customer behaviour.

For more sophisticated data analysis, pharmaceutical representatives can turn to dedicated business intelligence (BI) tools like Tableau or Power BI. These platforms allow users to create interactive dashboards that provide real-time insights into sales performance, market dynamics, and customer engagement. By visualizing data through these tools, representatives can identify patterns and correlations that may not be immediately apparent in raw data formats. Additionally, BI tools can integrate with other systems to pull data from various sources, enabling a more comprehensive view of the market landscape.

Another crucial area is the utilization of customer relationship management (CRM) systems, which are essential for managing interactions with healthcare providers. CRMs not only store essential contact information but also track engagement history, sales performance, and customer preferences. By analyzing this data, representatives can tailor their approaches to individual healthcare providers, fostering stronger relationships and ultimately enhancing sales effectiveness. Combining CRM insights with external market data can lead to more strategic decision-making and better targeting of marketing efforts.

Finally, advancements in artificial intelligence (AI) and machine learning (ML) are revolutionizing data analysis in the pharmaceutical industry. These technologies can analyze vast amounts of data quickly and accurately, identifying trends and making predictions that inform sales strategies. By integrating AI-driven analytics, representatives can enhance their ability to anticipate market shifts and respond proactively. As the pharmaceutical landscape continues to evolve, staying abreast of these tools and technologies will be crucial for representatives seeking to maintain a competitive edge and drive their success in the field.

Interpreting Data for Improved Sales Strategies

Interpreting data effectively is crucial for developing improved sales strategies within the pharmaceutical industry. Sales and marketing representatives must recognize that data is more than just numbers; it is a narrative that reveals trends, customer behaviors, and market dynamics. By analyzing this data, representatives can tailor their approaches to meet the specific needs of healthcare providers, ultimately enhancing their sales effectiveness. Understanding the nuances of data interpretation is therefore a fundamental skill for anyone looking to succeed in this competitive field.

One of the primary sources of data comes from sales performance metrics. By evaluating these metrics, representatives can identify which products are performing well and which are not. This analysis should extend beyond merely looking at the numbers; it involves digging deeper into the reasons behind sales trends. For instance, if a particular medication shows a decline in sales, understanding the underlying factors such as competitive pressures, changes in prescribing habits, or shifts in patient demographics can help formulate targeted strategies. This approach allows representatives to make informed decisions about where to focus their efforts and resources.

Another key aspect of data interpretation is understanding customer feedback and market research. Engaging with healthcare providers and gathering qualitative data can provide insights into their needs and preferences. By integrating this qualitative data with quantitative sales figures, representatives can develop a more holistic view of the market landscape. This dual approach not only aids in recognizing emerging trends but also enhances the ability to anticipate customer needs.
Representatives who actively seek and analyze this information will be better positioned to build effective relationships with healthcare providers and establish themselves as trusted partners.

Furthermore, leveraging advanced analytics tools can significantly enhance data interpretation. Many organizations now utilize sophisticated software that can process large volumes of data and generate actionable insights. By employing these tools, sales representatives can uncover patterns that may not be immediately apparent through manual analysis. For example, predictive analytics can forecast future sales trends based on historical data, enabling representatives to proactively adjust their strategies. Familiarity with these technologies equips sales teams to navigate the complexities of the pharmaceutical market more adeptly.

Finally, the importance of continuous learning cannot be overstated in the context of data interpretation. The pharmaceutical landscape is constantly evolving, and so too are the tools and techniques for analyzing data. Sales representatives and managers must commit to ongoing training and professional development to stay abreast of the latest methodologies and technologies in data analytics. By fostering a culture of learning and adaptability, organizations can ensure that their teams are well-equipped to interpret data effectively, thereby driving improved sales strategies and achieving long-term success in the pharmaceutical industry.

Chapter 10: Understanding Market Access and Reimbursement Strategies

Overview of Market Access in Pharma

Market access in the pharmaceutical industry is a critical component that determines how effectively a drug reaches patients. It encompasses a series of strategic activities aimed at ensuring that new therapies can enter the market and become accessible to the appropriate patient populations. This process involves navigating a complex landscape that includes regulatory approvals, pricing negotiations, and reimbursement frameworks. For sales and marketing representatives, understanding the intricacies of market access is essential for effectively communicating the value of their products to healthcare providers and payers.

At its core, market access strategies involve a comprehensive understanding of healthcare systems and the various stakeholders within them. These stakeholders include government agencies, private insurers, healthcare providers, and patients. Each group has distinct interests and requirements that must be addressed to facilitate a smooth entry for new pharmaceutical products. Sales representatives need to grasp how decisions made by these stakeholders can impact product availability and, consequently, sales performance.

This knowledge allows representatives to tailor their approach, focusing on the specific needs and concerns of each group and forging stronger relationships.

Reimbursement plays a pivotal role in market access, as it directly influences the financial viability of a drug in the market. Pharmaceutical companies must engage in negotiations with payers to establish pricing that reflects the drug's value while also being acceptable to the market. This process often requires robust evidence demonstrating clinical efficacy and cost-effectiveness. Medical representatives should be proficient in articulating this value proposition to healthcare providers, emphasizing how their product can contribute to improved patient outcomes and potentially reduce overall healthcare costs.

Additionally, regulatory compliance is a fundamental aspect of market access that cannot be overlooked. Representatives must be well-versed in the laws and guidelines governing pharmaceutical marketing and sales to avoid pitfalls that could jeopardize their company's ability to market a product. Understanding regulatory requirements helps ensure that communications with healthcare providers are accurate and compliant, fostering trust and credibility in the eyes of both providers and patients. This compliance is essential not only for ethical reasons but also for maintaining a competitive edge in a tightly regulated industry.

In conclusion, the landscape of market access in the pharmaceutical sector is multifaceted and requires a strategic approach from sales and marketing representatives. By developing a thorough understanding of market access principles, including stakeholder engagement, reimbursement processes, and regulatory compliance, representatives can enhance their effectiveness in the field. As they build relationships with healthcare providers and navigate the complexities of the market, their ability to communicate the value of their products will ultimately drive success in pharmaceutical sales.

This knowledge not only empowers representatives but also positions them as trusted partners in the healthcare ecosystem, facilitating better patient access to innovative therapies.

Key Components of Reimbursement Strategies

Reimbursement strategies are critical in ensuring that pharmaceutical products reach patients effectively and sustainably. Understanding the key components of these strategies is essential for sales and marketing representatives in the pharmaceutical industry. These components include pricing, access, and value demonstration, all of which work in concert to facilitate the reimbursement process. By mastering these elements, representatives can better position their products in an increasingly competitive market while also addressing the needs of healthcare providers and patients.

Pricing is the first essential component of reimbursement strategies. It involves setting a price for a pharmaceutical product that reflects its value while remaining competitive within the marketplace. This requires an understanding of various pricing models, including cost-plus pricing and value-based pricing. Sales representatives must be equipped with knowledge about how their product's price compares with similar therapies and be prepared to communicate this effectively to healthcare providers and payers.

A well-structured pricing strategy not only influences reimbursement decisions but also affects overall market access.

Access is another critical component linked to reimbursement strategies. This refers to the ability of patients and healthcare providers to obtain a pharmaceutical product. Key factors influencing access include formulary placements, prior authorization requirements, and patient assistance programs. Medical representatives should be proactive in understanding the access landscape for their products and educating healthcare providers about the steps needed to secure coverage. Building strong relationships with payers and engaging in discussions about access can enhance the likelihood of favourable reimbursement outcomes.

Value demonstration is the third pillar of effective reimbursement strategies. It involves providing evidence that a pharmaceutical product offers significant benefits compared to existing therapies. This can include clinical trial results, real-world evidence, and health economic studies that highlight improved patient outcomes or cost savings. Sales representatives must be adept at articulating this value proposition to various stakeholders, including healthcare providers, payers, and patients. By effectively communicating the value of their products, representatives can facilitate positive reimbursement decisions and enhance market acceptance.

In conclusion, a comprehensive understanding of pricing, access, and value demonstration can significantly enhance reimbursement strategies for pharmaceutical products. Sales and marketing representatives must integrate these components into their daily practices to navigate the complexities of the healthcare landscape successfully. By doing so, they can not only drive sales but also contribute to better patient outcomes and overall success in the pharmaceutical industry. Developing expertise in these areas will empower representatives to advocate for their products effectively and ultimately support the broader mission of improving healthcare access and quality.

Collaborating with Payers and Stakeholders

Collaborating with payers and stakeholders is crucial for pharmaceutical representatives aiming to achieve success in a competitive marketplace. Understanding the roles of various stakeholders, including insurance companies, pharmacy benefit managers, and healthcare providers, can significantly influence the acceptance and success of a pharmaceutical product. Building relationships with these entities requires a strategic approach that emphasizes mutual benefits. By aligning the interests of payers with the therapeutic value of their products, representatives can facilitate smoother market access and enhance the overall value proposition of their offerings.

Effective communication is key when engaging with payers and stakeholders. Representatives should focus on conveying clinical and economic data that highlights the benefits of their products, not just for patients but also for the healthcare system at large. This involves presenting compelling evidence regarding treatment outcomes, cost-effectiveness, and the overall impact on patient care.

By tailoring their messaging to address the specific concerns and objectives of payers, representatives can foster trust and establish themselves as credible partners in improving healthcare delivery.

In addition to communication, understanding the nuances of market access and reimbursement strategies is essential. Representatives must be well-versed in the processes that payers use to evaluate new therapies and the criteria that influence formulary decisions. This knowledge allows representatives to anticipate potential barriers to access and address them proactively. Engaging in dialogue with payers about their priorities and challenges can lead to collaborative solutions that benefit both parties, ultimately improving patient access to necessary treatments.

Training and development programs play a vital role in equipping pharmaceutical representatives with the skills needed to navigate these complex interactions. By investing in ongoing education regarding payer dynamics, representatives can better understand the landscape in which they operate. Workshops, seminars, and online courses focused on negotiation strategies, economic modelling, and stakeholder engagement can greatly enhance a representative's effectiveness. Continuous learning ensures that representatives remain current with industry trends and payer requirements, allowing them to adapt their strategies accordingly.

Lastly, leveraging data and analytics is an indispensable component of successful collaboration with payers and stakeholders. By analyzing market trends, payer behaviors, and patient outcomes, representatives can formulate strategies that are data-driven and evidence-based. This not only enhances their credibility but also provides actionable insights that can drive discussions with payers. Utilizing data effectively can help representatives identify opportunities for collaboration, tailor their approaches to meet specific stakeholder needs, and ultimately contribute to the broader goal of improving patient access to innovative therapies.

Chapter 11: Training and Development Programs for Medical Reps

Importance of Ongoing Training

Ongoing training is a cornerstone of success in the pharmaceutical industry, especially for sales and marketing representatives. The rapidly evolving landscape of pharmaceuticals demands that professionals remain current with the latest developments in drug formulations, therapeutic areas, and regulatory changes.

Continuous education not only enhances product knowledge but also equips representatives with the skills needed to engage effectively with healthcare providers. As the complexity of healthcare increases, representatives who commit to lifelong learning can articulate the value of their products more convincingly, thereby fostering trust and credibility within their networks.

The importance of ongoing training extends beyond product knowledge; it encompasses the mastery of sales techniques that are essential for success. The pharmaceutical market is characterized by fierce competition, requiring representatives to differentiate themselves through effective communication and relationship-building skills. Regular training sessions provide an opportunity to refine these techniques, learn new strategies, and share best practices among peers.

This collaborative environment fosters a culture of excellence, where representatives can learn from each other's experiences and insights, ultimately enhancing their performance in the field.

Regulatory compliance is another critical aspect that underscores the necessity of ongoing training. The pharmaceutical industry is heavily regulated, and the repercussions of non-compliance can be severe, including legal penalties and damage to reputation. Training programs that focus on the nuances of regulatory guidelines ensure that representatives are well-versed in compliance issues. This knowledge not only protects the organization but also empowers representatives to conduct their business ethically and responsibly, positioning them as trustworthy partners to healthcare professionals.

In addition to enhancing individual capabilities, ongoing training also plays a vital role in leveraging data and analytics for informed decision-making. As the industry increasingly relies on data-driven insights to shape marketing strategies and sales approaches, representatives must be adept at interpreting and utilizing this information. Training programs that emphasize data literacy can help representatives understand market trends, customer preferences, and the effectiveness of their sales tactics. This analytical perspective allows them to tailor their approach, leading to more successful engagements with healthcare providers.

Finally, investing in ongoing training is essential for career advancement within the pharmaceutical sector. As representatives develop their skills and knowledge, they become more valuable assets to their organizations. Companies that prioritize training demonstrate a commitment to their employees' professional growth, which can enhance job satisfaction and retention. For individuals, continuous learning opens doors to new opportunities, whether in management roles or specialized positions within the industry. A culture of ongoing training not only drives personal success but also contributes to the overall success of the organization in the competitive pharmaceutical landscape.

Types of Training Programs Available

In the pharmaceutical industry, effective training programs are essential for equipping sales and marketing representatives with the necessary skills and knowledge to thrive. Various types of training programs cater to the diverse needs of medical representatives, focusing on different aspects of their roles. These programs typically encompass product knowledge training, sales techniques development, compliance education, and digital marketing strategies, all of which play a critical role in enhancing performance and achieving success in the competitive landscape of pharma sales.

Product knowledge training is foundational for any medical representative. This type of training ensures that representatives are well-versed in the features, benefits, and mechanisms of action of the products they promote. Understanding the science behind pharmaceuticals allows representatives to confidently engage with healthcare providers, address their inquiries, and provide evidence-based information.

Furthermore, continuous updates on new products, formulations, or indications are essential to maintain relevance in discussions with healthcare professionals, ensuring that representatives can advocate effectively for their offerings.

Sales techniques development programs focus on enhancing interpersonal skills and adopting best practices in selling. These programs often cover various methodologies, including consultative selling, relationship-building strategies, and objection handling. By learning to tailor their approach to the unique needs of different healthcare providers, representatives can foster stronger relationships and drive sales performance. Role-playing scenarios and real-world simulations are commonly incorporated into these training sessions, allowing participants to practice and refine their skills in a supportive environment.

Compliance education is another vital aspect of training for pharmaceutical representatives. Given the stringent regulatory framework governing the industry, sales teams must understand the laws and guidelines that dictate their interactions with healthcare professionals. Training programs focused on regulatory compliance ensure that representatives are aware of the ethical considerations and legal obligations that inform their marketing practices. This knowledge not only protects the company from potential legal issues but also builds credibility and trust with healthcare providers.

In today's digital landscape, incorporating digital marketing strategies into training programs is becoming increasingly important. As more healthcare providers engage with digital channels, representatives must be adept at utilizing these platforms to reach their audience effectively. Training in digital tools, social media engagement, and online analytics equips sales teams with the skills necessary to navigate the evolving market dynamics. By leveraging data and analytics, representatives can gain insights into customer behavior and preferences, enabling them to tailor their outreach and maximize their impact in the field.

Measuring the Effectiveness of Training

Measuring the effectiveness of training in the pharmaceutical industry is crucial for ensuring that sales and marketing representatives are equipped with the skills and knowledge necessary to succeed in a highly competitive environment. The effectiveness of training programs can significantly influence not only the performance of individual representatives but also the overall success of the organization. To gauge the impact of training initiatives, companies must establish clear metrics that align with their business objectives. This includes assessing changes in sales performance, improved compliance with regulatory standards, and the ability to build effective relationships with healthcare providers.

One effective approach to measuring training effectiveness is through the use of the Kirkpatrick Model, which evaluates training based on four levels: reaction, learning, behavior, and results. At the first level, organizations can gather feedback from participants regarding their perceptions of the training experience. This initial reaction can provide insights into the training's relevance and engagement level. The second level assesses the knowledge and skills acquired during the training. Pre- and post-training assessments can be conducted to evaluate the knowledge gained and to ensure that representatives understand the therapeutic areas and products they will be promoting.

The third level of the Kirkpatrick Model focuses on behavior change in the workplace. This involves observing how training translates into on-the-job performance. For pharmaceutical representatives, this could mean monitoring their interactions with healthcare providers and assessing whether they employ the techniques learned during training. Regular performance reviews and one-on-one coaching sessions can provide valuable insights into how representatives are applying their training in real-world scenarios. Engaging managers in this process is essential, as they play a critical role in reinforcing training concepts and providing ongoing support.

The final level of the Kirkpatrick Model evaluates the overall results of the training program, which can be quantified through sales metrics, market share growth, and customer satisfaction scores. By analyzing these outcomes, pharmaceutical companies can determine the return on investment for their training initiatives. Additionally, tracking long-term performance trends can help identify areas for improvement and inform future training programs. This continuous feedback loop ensures that training efforts remain aligned with evolving market dynamics and organizational goals.

In conclusion, the measurement of training effectiveness in the pharmaceutical industry is a multifaceted process that requires ongoing evaluation and adaptation. By employing structured models like the Kirkpatrick Model and utilizing a combination of qualitative and quantitative metrics, organizations can ensure their training programs are impactful and aligned with their strategic objectives. Ultimately, effective training leads to improved performance among sales representatives, fosters stronger relationships with healthcare providers, and contributes to the overall success of the pharmaceutical organization.

Chapter 12: Exploring Career Advancement Opportunities in Pharma Sales

Career Paths in the Pharmaceutical Industry

Career paths in the pharmaceutical industry offer diverse opportunities for sales and marketing representatives and managers, each with unique roles and responsibilities. As the industry evolves, professionals can explore various paths that align with their skills and aspirations. For medical representatives, starting as a field sales representative can provide foundational knowledge of products, client interactions, and market dynamics. This role typically involves extensive travel, direct engagement with healthcare providers, and an emphasis on building lasting relationships, which is crucial for success in this sector.

As representatives gain experience, they may pursue positions in product management or brand management. These roles focus on strategizing marketing initiatives, analyzing market trends, and collaborating with cross-functional teams to launch and promote pharmaceutical products effectively. Understanding customer needs and market access strategies becomes essential in these positions as representatives work to ensure that their products reach the intended audiences.

Additionally, mastering communication skills and therapeutic expertise can enhance the effectiveness of marketing campaigns and contribute to overall brand success.

Another promising avenue is the move into regulatory affairs or compliance roles, where professionals ensure that all marketing practices adhere to industry regulations and ethical standards. As the pharmaceutical landscape becomes increasingly complex with changing regulations, expertise in navigating compliance is invaluable. This path not only requires a thorough understanding of legal frameworks but also the ability to communicate these regulations clearly to both internal teams and external stakeholders, thereby safeguarding the company's reputation and product integrity.

For those with a passion for data, positions in market research and analytics are critical in shaping sales strategies and understanding customer behaviors. Utilizing data analytics allows professionals to identify emerging market trends, assess competition, and optimize sales approaches. As digital marketing strategies continue to evolve, leveraging data to drive targeted campaigns and improve engagement with healthcare providers is becoming a fundamental skill set for success in pharmaceutical sales.

Finally, career advancement opportunities in the pharmaceutical industry can lead to leadership roles, such as sales manager or director of sales and marketing. These positions require a comprehensive understanding of the industry, strong leadership capabilities, and the ability to mentor and develop junior representatives. Continuous learning through training and development programs is essential for staying abreast of industry changes, ensuring representatives not only excel in their current roles but are also prepared to take on greater responsibilities in the future. By navigating these pathways, professionals can cultivate a rewarding career in the dynamic pharmaceutical sector.

Skills Needed for Advancement

To thrive and advance in the pharmaceutical industry, sales and marketing representatives must possess a diverse skill set tailored to the unique demands of their roles. A fundamental skill is the ability to build and maintain effective relationships with healthcare providers. This involves not only establishing trust but also understanding the needs and preferences of the providers.

Representatives must be adept at active listening, empathy, and interpersonal communication, as these skills facilitate meaningful dialogues that can lead to successful partnerships and increased product adoption.

Another crucial competency is mastering pharmaceutical sales techniques. This encompasses a deep understanding of the sales process, from prospecting to closing deals. Successful representatives need to be skilled negotiators, capable of presenting products persuasively and addressing objections effectively. Training in consultative selling techniques can empower representatives to position products as solutions to specific healthcare challenges, thereby enhancing their overall effectiveness in the field. Continuous practice and refinement of these techniques are essential, as the landscape of pharmaceutical sales is ever-evolving.

In addition to interpersonal skills and sales techniques, a solid grasp of regulatory compliance is paramount. The pharmaceutical industry is heavily regulated, and sales representatives must be well-versed in guidelines that govern marketing practices and interactions with healthcare professionals. Understanding the boundaries of permissible promotional activities not only protects the company from legal ramifications but also fosters ethical selling practices. Ongoing education in regulatory changes is vital for representatives to remain compliant and maintain credibility in their interactions with healthcare providers.

Digital marketing strategies also play a crucial role in the advancement of a medical representative's career. As the landscape shifts towards digital engagement, representatives must be proficient in leveraging various digital tools and platforms to reach their audience effectively. This includes understanding social media, email marketing, and content creation tailored to healthcare professionals. By harnessing these digital strategies, representatives can enhance their reach, engage with stakeholders more effectively, and ultimately drive better sales outcomes.

Finally, a commitment to continuous learning and professional development is essential for career advancement in the pharmaceutical sector. Engaging in training programs and seeking out mentorship opportunities can significantly enhance a representative's knowledge and skills. Investing in product knowledge, therapeutic expertise, and data analytics can empower representatives to make informed decisions and provide valuable insights to healthcare providers. As the pharmaceutical industry continues to evolve, those who prioritize their development will be better positioned to seize opportunities and achieve long-term success in their careers.

Networking and Mentorship Opportunities

Networking and mentorship opportunities are crucial components of a successful career in the pharmaceutical industry. For sales and marketing representatives and managers, these relationships can significantly enhance professional growth and open doors to new avenues. Establishing a solid network within the industry allows representatives to connect with healthcare providers, colleagues, and key opinion leaders. This interaction not only facilitates the sharing of knowledge and best practices but also creates a platform for discussing challenges and solutions that are pertinent to pharmaceutical sales.

Mentorship plays a vital role in navigating the complexities of the pharmaceutical landscape. A mentor, often a seasoned professional, can provide invaluable insights into effective sales techniques, product knowledge, and therapeutic expertise. Engaging with a mentor allows representatives to learn from their experiences and avoid common pitfalls. Moreover, mentors can offer guidance on regulatory compliance and market access strategies, which are essential for successfully positioning products in a competitive market. This relationship fosters personal and professional development, empowering representatives to achieve their career aspirations.

In addition to one-on-one mentorship, participating in industry events and conferences can significantly expand a representative's professional network. These gatherings provide an excellent opportunity to meet peers, share experiences, and learn about the latest trends in pharmaceutical marketing and sales. Engaging in workshops and panel discussions allows representatives to gain insights from industry leaders and experts. Furthermore, these interactions can lead to potential collaborations and partnerships that can enhance one's effectiveness in the field.

Utilizing digital platforms for networking has become increasingly important in today's pharmaceutical landscape. Social media networks, professional groups, and online forums offer representatives the chance to connect with a broader audience. By actively participating in discussions and sharing valuable content, representatives can establish themselves as thought leaders in their niche. This online presence not only enhances visibility but also creates opportunities for mentorship and collaboration with professionals from diverse backgrounds and specialties.

Finally, organizations should encourage a culture of networking and mentorship within their teams. Implementing structured mentorship programs and facilitating networking events can help representatives build relationships that foster growth and success. Encouraging team members to share knowledge and experiences creates an environment of continuous learning, which is critical in the ever-evolving pharmaceutical industry. By prioritizing networking and mentorship, both individuals and organizations can drive performance and achieve lasting success in the competitive world of pharmaceutical sales.

Chapter 13: Conclusion and Future Outlook

Recap of Key Themes

In "Pharmaceutical Success: A Medical Representative's Roadmap," several key themes emerge that are crucial for sales and marketing representatives and managers in the pharmaceutical industry. One of the primary themes is the importance of building effective relationships with healthcare providers. Trust and rapport with physicians and other healthcare professionals are foundational to successful sales.

Representatives must prioritize understanding the needs and concerns of healthcare providers, actively listening to their feedback, and providing valuable information that supports their clinical decisions. This relationship-building approach not only enhances sales opportunities but also contributes to better patient outcomes.

Another significant theme is the mastery of pharmaceutical sales techniques. Representatives need to develop a comprehensive understanding of various sales methodologies, including consultative selling and solution-based approaches. Adapting these techniques to fit the specific needs of different healthcare settings can lead to more effective engagement with providers. Training in negotiation skills and objection handling is also critical, as these abilities enable representatives to navigate challenging discussions and secure buy-in from healthcare professionals. Continuous practice and refinement of these skills are vital for maintaining a competitive edge in the market.

Navigating regulatory compliance is another core theme that cannot be overlooked. The pharmaceutical industry is heavily regulated, and representatives must stay updated on the latest laws and guidelines. Understanding the compliance landscape helps mitigate risks and ensures that promotional activities adhere to legal standards. This knowledge not only protects the company but also enhances the credibility of the representative in the eyes of healthcare providers. A strong grasp of compliance issues empowers representatives to engage in ethical marketing practices while effectively promoting their products.

Digital marketing strategies have become increasingly important in the pharmaceutical sector. As healthcare providers become more tech-savvy, utilizing digital channels for outreach and education is essential. Representatives should leverage social media, email campaigns, and digital content to reach their target audience effectively. Understanding analytics tools and metrics is key to measuring the success of these strategies and making data-driven adjustments to marketing efforts. By embracing digital marketing, representatives can enhance their visibility and foster deeper engagement with healthcare providers.

Lastly, career advancement opportunities within the pharmaceutical sales sector represent a vital theme for both new and seasoned representatives. Ongoing training and development programs are crucial for personal and professional growth. Emphasizing the importance of mentorship and networking can help individuals identify pathways to advancement within their organizations. Investing in continuous learning not only enhances individual capabilities but also contributes to a more skilled and effective sales force. As the pharmaceutical landscape continues to evolve, those who prioritize their development will find greater success in their careers.

The Future of Pharmaceutical Sales

The pharmaceutical sales landscape is on the brink of major changes, influenced by technological advancements, shifting healthcare environments, and evolving consumer behaviors.

It is essential for sales and marketing representatives, as well as managers in the pharmaceutical field, to keep pace with these trends to stay competitive. One of the most significant advancements is the incorporation of artificial intelligence and machine learning into sales processes. These technologies allow representatives to process large volumes of data to pinpoint potential leads, comprehend physician preferences, and customize their strategies accordingly.

This data-driven approach not only improves interactions with healthcare providers but also boosts the effectiveness of sales tactics.

Digital marketing strategies are increasingly becoming central to pharmaceutical sales efforts. With the growing reliance on digital platforms by healthcare providers and patients alike, representatives must leverage social media, email campaigns, and online content to foster relationships and communicate product value. The shift to digital engagement requires representatives to develop robust digital literacy skills and an understanding of how to create engaging, informative content that resonates with their audience. Embracing these strategies will empower representatives to connect with healthcare professionals in meaningful ways that traditional methods may not achieve.

Furthermore, navigating regulatory compliance continues to be a critical aspect of pharmaceutical sales. As regulations evolve, sales teams must stay informed and adapt their strategies to ensure compliance while still effectively promoting their products. This involves not only understanding the current regulatory landscape but also anticipating future changes that may impact sales practices. Continuous training and development programs focused on compliance will equip sales representatives with the knowledge necessary to operate within legal parameters while driving sales success.

Building vibrant relationships with healthcare providers is essential in the pharmaceutical industry! The future of these connections will undoubtedly depend on a profound understanding of what providers truly need and prefer. Sales representatives who dedicate time to cultivating these relationships through engaging, personalized interactions and regular follow-ups will experience remarkable success. The focus on trust and credibility will be crucial as healthcare providers look for partners who can offer not just products but also invaluable insights and support that enhance patient care!

The evolution of pharmaceutical sales is poised for significant influence from advancements in market access and reimbursement strategies. As the healthcare landscape grows more complex, representatives need to thoroughly understand market access dynamics and reimbursement processes. By mastering these challenges, sales teams can effectively position their products in the market, aligning with both patient needs and business objectives. Embracing these exciting changes and continually enhancing their skills will prepare sales and marketing representatives to thrive in the future of pharmaceutical sales

Final Thoughts on Achieving Success in Pharma Sales

Achieving success in pharmaceutical sales requires a multifaceted approach that integrates various skills, knowledge, and strategies. As the industry continues to evolve, it is vital for sales and marketing representatives, along with managers, to remain adaptable and proactive in their efforts. The journey to success involves not only mastering sales techniques but also building effective relationships with healthcare providers and understanding the complexities of regulatory compliance. By focusing on these critical areas, sales professionals can position themselves as trusted partners in the healthcare ecosystem.

Building strong relationships with healthcare providers is fundamental to driving successful sales outcomes. Engaging with physicians, pharmacists, and other healthcare professionals requires a deep understanding of their needs and challenges. By demonstrating genuine interest and offering valuable insights, sales representatives can foster trust and credibility. This relationship-building approach not only enhances the likelihood of successful sales but also contributes to improved patient outcomes, aligning the goals of healthcare providers with those of the pharmaceutical company.

Another key aspect of success in pharma sales is the continuous development of product knowledge and therapeutic expertise. Sales representatives must be well-versed in the products they promote, including their clinical benefits, potential side effects, and competitive positioning. This knowledge empowers representatives to have informed discussions with healthcare providers, addressing their questions and concerns effectively. Furthermore, ongoing education and training programs can help sales teams stay updated on industry trends, new product launches, and regulatory changes, ensuring they remain competitive in the field.

In today's digital age, utilizing digital marketing strategies is essential for reaching target audiences effectively. Sales representatives should leverage digital tools and platforms to enhance their outreach and engagement. This includes utilizing social media, email campaigns, and webinars to disseminate information about products and industry updates. By integrating traditional sales techniques with modern digital strategies, representatives can create a more comprehensive approach to their sales efforts, ultimately leading to increased visibility and accessibility for healthcare providers.

Lastly, leveraging data and analytics is crucial for understanding market dynamics and decision-making processes in pharmaceutical sales. Sales representatives and managers should harness data to identify trends, track performance metrics, and evaluate the effectiveness of their strategies. This analytical approach enables teams to make informed decisions and adapt their tactics based on real-world insights. By fostering a culture of continuous learning and improvement, pharmaceutical sales professionals can navigate the complexities of the industry and drive sustained success in their careers.

Thank You

Maples
Book Solutions

Enjoyed this book?

Positive reviews from awesome customers like you
help others to feel confident about choosing
Maples Book Solutions too.

Could you take **60 seconds** to go to Amazon platform
and share your happy experiences?

We will be forever grateful.
Thank you in advance for helping us out!

www.ingramcontent.com/pod-product-compliance
Lightning Source LLC
Chambersburg PA
CBHW071514220526
45472CB00003B/1022